NEVER SOLVE A NON-PROBLEM

The Entrepreneur's Handbook

Tony Carter
Matt Guercia
Nora Minor

Writers Club Press
San Jose · New York · Lincoln · Shanghai

Never Solve A Non-Problem, the entrepreneur's handbook
Copyright © 1999 by Tony Carter

Illustrations Copyright © by Matt Guercia

No part of this book may be reproduced, stored in a retrieval system or distributed, in whole or in part, in print or by any other means, electronic, mechanical, photocopying, recording, or otherwise without the written permission of the author.

To discuss this book with the author, contact Tony Carter at Edge Technonogies, Inc., 8245 Boone Boulevard, Suite 704, Vienna, VA 22182, or email tony.carter@edgetechnologies.com.

For information about wholesale distribution, bulk sales or use of these images for any other purpose, send email to receptionist@edgetechnologies.com, or send correspondence to Edge Technonogies, Inc., 8245 Boone Boulevard, Suite 704, Vienna, VA 22182, telephone 703-288-9770, fax 703-288-9775.

Visit our Web site at www.edgetechnologies.com for more information.

ISBN: 1-893652-28-9

This book was published using the on-line/on-demand publishing services of Writers Club Press, an imprint of iUniverse, Inc.

For information address:
iUniverse.com, Inc.
620 North 48th Street
Suite 201
Lincoln, NE 68504-3467
www.iUniverse.com

URL: http://www.writersclub.com

For
Sue
Simon
Ben
Sam

Entrepreneuring is fun but the love of a family is the greatest fun of all.

THANKS

My special thanks to Matt Guercia and Nora Minor. I have never met them but have worked with them through that wonderful media "the net".

My thanks to Dr. Jack London, Chairman and CEO of CACI for allowing me to use material from the CACI management manual. Thanks to Keith Waite of the London Times and special thanks to some of the great entrepreneurs I have worked with...Dr. Bill Fain, Willi Erich, Cor Swart, Shaun Boyle, John Wyatt, The Supersonic Boomers: Ted Hooban, Julie and Mellissa McKinnon (now with CD Now), Jeff Gordon with IXL, John Harris with Technology 2000 and the "chip off the old block" my son Simon Carter.

FOREWORD

This book is intended to be an entrepreneur's management manual. It contains a collection of ideas that are practical and essential to business success.

The book is a compilation of ideas pulled from many sources, very few are original to the author. The inspiration for many of them came from Peter Drucker and the Late Herb Karr, founder and chairman of CACI. Some came from Townsend and others from experience and people we have worked with. The inspiration for the cartoons have come from several sources notably Virgil Parche and Keith Waite of the London Times.

The ideas and notions presented here are not completely original but have been described differently and reinvented thousands of times in different languages all over the world.

None of the "homilies" are absolute truths applicable under all conditions. Many of course are over simplifications ignoring certain factors. They may sometimes be ignored but never ignored safely. They must certainly be used carefully. The "homilies" contain contradictions and the entrepreneur must understand that contradictory principles can simultaneously be valid and that it is often necessary to strike a balance between these conflicting requirements.

The ideas presented here should not be forgotten in our day-to-day work which must be fun.

Of course the internet, the Web, are changing many of these values. Believe me, the rush to market share, the mania for "eyeballs" will, over the next three to four years, revert to form and to the intrinsic values that businesses have been built on for generations. Revenue and profit are all pervasive. Wall Street will prevail even if at the moment they don't understand. However, for the entrepreneur "Seize The Day" entrepreneuring can be fun, the Industrial Revolution will transition into the information age.

THE ENTREPRENEUR'S 10 COMMANDMENTS

COMMANDMENT 1

"Thou Shalt Honor Thy People All The Days Of Their Life (With The Company)"

People are your number one asset -- make them your number one priority. Value them, listen to them, pay attention to them.

Never Solve A Non-Problem

COMMANDMENT II

"Thou Shalt Stay Close To Thy Customer"

Know your customer, stay in touch with them, never hand them over to someone else.

COMMANDMENT III

"Thou Shalt Seize The Day Every Day"

Look for the opportunities every day brings. Finish things. Make life exciting.

Never Solve A Non-Problem

COMMANDMENT IV

"Honor Thy Enterprise"

Never run your company down to anyone. Be a cheerleader while constantly looking for improvement. Suggest to the boss and employees new things that can be made better.

COMMANDMENT V

"Thou Shalt Share Rewards Among Everyone in The Enterprise"

Reward everyone. Be generous with shares. Allow everyone the opportunity to own a piece of the company -- to have a stake in its success.

Never Solve A Non-Problem

COMMANDMENT VI

"Thou Shalt Not Adulterate Thy Competence"

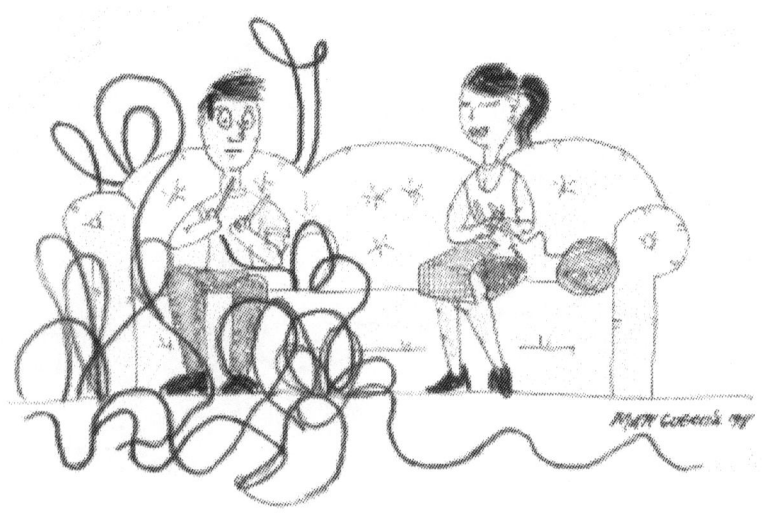

Do what you're good at and encourage others to live up to their best potential. Recruit people who are better than you in other areas.

COMMANDMENT VII

"Thou Shalt Fish or Cut Bait"

Speed is essential. Procrastination kills. Act now.

Never Solve A Non-Problem

COMMANDMENT VIII

"Thou Shalt Not Commit Complexity"

Don't overcomplicate. Avoid paralysis by analysis.

COMMANDMENT IX and X

"Thou Shalt Worship Two Gods: Quality and Profit"

Never compromise on quality. Remember, profit is the true measure of how well the company is doing. Quality delivers profit.

Never Solve A Non-Problem

THE HOMILIES ON MANAGEMENT

NEVER SOLVE A NON-PROBLEM

NEVER SOLVE A NON-PROBLEM

One of the worst things any budding entrepreneur can do is waste time solving non-problems. Non-problems come under the heading of things that haven't happened yet and may never happen. Solving problems that don't exist is a far worse waste of time and money than working on an unavoidable problem.

As an entrepreneur you must be in the position to answer the "what if" question. If you foresee a possible difficulty, before you rush into solving it, ask yourself, "Could I solve this problem after it arises? (If it ever does!) Would I have time to do so?"

In most cases, the answer is yes.

Granted, the future is uncertain, so some contingency planning in business is always necessary. At the same time , keep in mind that most contingencies should not be planned for because *the number of possible contingencies is infinite.* Plan properly and in detail, and make your plans happen, so you will never have to answer the question, "What on Earth will we do now?"

Mary was awake all night worrying about the events of the following day. C Corp's check was late, and if it wasn't in the office in the morning, it would be difficult to make payroll that week. To make matters worse, if the D Corp order wasn't won, everyone would be on "dead" time next month. Mary worked herself into such a state she didn't go to sleep until 6a.m. She was late into the office and missed Jane's celebration. Jane had visited C Corp and collected the check, and on her way back to the office had called D Corp to collect the purchase order. Mary had worried where Jane had acted.

MAKE THINGS HAPPEN

MAKE THINGS HAPPEN

The difference between failure and success is the difference between thinking and talking about something and actually making it happen.

Taking action comes hard to some people. Somehow meeting after meeting and being in the endless process of getting ready comes much easier. These people are not entrepreneurs – they mostly belong in the hierarchy of bureaucratic enterprises.

The true entrepreneur, on the other hand, is proactive. Any good entrepreneur will first decide on the result wanted, and will proceed to think through in detail the sequence of actions required to arrive at that result. They then march relentlessly through the detailed steps required to reach their goals, "picking them up and laying them down" as they go along.

Decide on your target and ask yourself what it will take to make it happen. And then *go do it.*

Rachel and Suzanne, chefs at a fine restaurant, talked often about leaving their jobs and beginning their own catering business. Doing a little research, they realized they would need a large amount of capital for start-up expenses. They also realized running their own company would require business and marketing skills in which they had no experience. Rachel balked at going into debt and was not willing to take on new responsibilities. But Suzanne pressed forward and soon found a silent partner willing to provide start-up costs in return for a portion of the profits. She also took classes in accounting and marketing offered at the local university, and hired a part-time consultant to help with the business details. Today she works for herself, while Rachel is still working for someone else.

**DIVERSIFICATION IS
THE ONLY PROTECTION AGAINST
AN UNKNOWN FAILURE**

DIVERSIFICATION IS THE ONLY PROTECTION AGAINST AN UNKNOWN FAILURE

For any entrepreneur, concentration on a small number of important items is the key to business success, but concentration without diversification can be fatal. Hanging by a single thread in any critical area – being dependent on a single customer, a single manager, a single business proposal, a single vendor – is extremely dangerous.

But diversification has its own risks. The entrepreneur who attempts to take his company into areas in which he has no expertise will often fail. A manager who sees vast potential in other geographical areas without the knowledge of how to benefit from it will often fail.

Instead, think building *as your diversification strategy. Build upon those areas you know; expand from your current base of products, services, people and markets.*

Build on what is successful and stick to what you know "how to." Build so you are not dependant on a single account, a single vendor, a single prospect. Build so you are never hanging by a single thread in any critical area.

Jack had built a successful business distributing cleaning products to the automotive industry. He had pretty much saturated his market, and was looking for ways to grow the business. He made the acquaintance of a chemist who offered to help Jack develop and manufacture his own line of cleaning products, which he could sell to his existing customers at a substantially higher profit than the products he was currently distributing. Jack made the investment to begin manufacturing, and, with his built-in customer base and solid knowledge of the industry, increased his profits by 30% the following year.

**DON'T ATTEMPT THINGS
THAT ARE TOO FAR OUTSIDE
THE REALM OF YOUR EXPERIENCE**

DON'T ATTEMPT THINGS THAT ARE TOO FAR OUTSIDE THE REALM OF YOUR EXPERIENCE

In the beginning, you concentrate on those things you do well and you compensate in those areas in which you are not as good by recruiting help. Then comes a time when you see opportunities in other areas. If you don't have the expertise, don't have the money; don't attempt them at all.

The management gurus all have different ways of expressing this.

Townsend says, "If you are attempting the impossible, you will fail." Peters & Waterman say "Stick to the knitting." And Heller tells you to "concentrate on what you do well."

Management is about that. But what about exploration, risk-taking, expansion and new markets? The best way to do it is to do it through others who can lead the way. If you can recruit people who are better than you, and build on their experience, then and only then can you, through others, attempt those things where you have no experience.

A British company, hoping to build in its success at home, opened small offices in Australia, Hong Kong and Singapore, and staffed them with British employees. The offices failed because they were outside the realm of the company's experience. Had they recruited local experts with experience in those markets, one of two things would have happened; they would have been warned not to proceed because the market conditions were not conducive, or they would have succeeded because the locals would have brought the right expertise to make the business thrive.

DO YOUR OWN DOG WORK

DO YOUR OWN DOG WORK

In other words, don't delegate.

Delegation is the most misunderstood word in management.

What typically happens is a manager will first create a position called "deputy". This in no way infers that the deputy has any authority; it nearly always means the deputy will carry out certain tasks the manager has no desire to do. If it goes wrong, the manager blames his deputy. If it goes right, the manager claims the credit.

Don't delegate.

You give and people accept/take/grab responsibility. With this responsibility, good people will grab the authority. This should happen at every stage of corporate growth.

At every level in the organization, give people complete things to do – not the bits you don't want. Then, try hard not to interfere. Help if you are asked, but only if asked. Step in only if you see it going horribly wrong.

Things will be accomplished, and you won't have delegated a thing.

Jane was great at making presentations, but she hated the follow-up. So she hired Laura to make follow-up calls. Business stagnated for several reasons, one being Laura really didn't have the benefit of the initial contact to build upon for follow-up, and another being clients sometimes resented Jane dropping out of the picture once they had begun to build a relationship with her. Laura suggested another approach – that she and Jane work the account as a team, with Laura being involved up front in the presentation work. Business improved immediately because Laura had assumed responsibility for the entire process, and gained new authority for serving clients.

ABANDON YOUR FAILURES EARLY

ABANDON YOUR FAILURES EARLY

How often have you heard, "We've put so much in, we might as well go on." If this is the only reason you have for continuing with a position, a product or a company, get out! You must be committed to your business and everything about it with your heart and soul — but don't be emotionally blind.

In his book, *The Business Of Winning*, Heller offers some suggestions on how to determine if it's time to fish or cut bait. He maintains the answer should lie in judgment, instinct and intuition, and also advocates asking yourself the following questions:

1. What is the worst possible outcome if I continue?
2. What is the likeliest outcome if I continue?
3. What is the best possible outcome if I continue?
4. Am I prepared to accept the outcome in #1?
5. Is the outcome in #2 worth having?
6. If not, is the outcome in #3 worth having?

Answer these questions. If the answers are NO to the last three, give up. You'll live to fight another day.

Venture Capitalist #1 invests in 10 companies, and soon finds six are succeeding and four are failing. He pulls the funding from the four who are struggling and reinvests the capital into making the other six thrive. Venture Capitalist #2 invests in 10 companies and experiences the same success/failure ratio. However, Venture Capitalist #2 pours more resources into the floundering companies to try to pump them up, leaving less capital to invest in the six who are doing well. Venture Capitalist #2 ends up with 10 companies — 4 failures and 6 moderate successes. Venture Capitalist #1 ends up with only 6 companies — but each of them is a real winner.

ALWAYS BOOTSTRAP

ALWAYS BOOTSTRAP

Dollars may be of equal value, but they are not all equally easy to get. As an entrepreneur, instill the concept of bootstrapping in all of your people. Educate them about the basic principle of business management: you can never afford to spend money out of capital.

Expenditures must be financed out of revenue, or skimmed off current profit — not by reducing capital. Capital dollars are as easy to spend as others, but they are at least 20 to 50 times as hard to attain as revenue dollars.

Insistence on bootstrapping can also help hold costs down to where a profit is possible. Most businesses who stay in business for an extended period of time started with a small amount of capital and bootstrapped from there. Many other businesses have started out by first raising a large amount of capital only to proceed to spend it — burning brightly on the way to bankruptcy.

By the time her third child was in daycare, Amy realized the back-pack and blanket and pillow she sent with her child every day was cumbersome. She designed a sleep sack with built-in pillow and carrying straps. When other mothers at the daycare center start asking Amy where she got her sleep sack, Amy knew she had a viable product, although she had very little capital to finance it. Rather, Amy took her prototype to every major daycare center in the city, and also to the headquarters of several daycare franchises. She got enough orders to finance her first factory shipment — and financed subsequent product shipments from previous ones. Within 2 years, Amy had built her business to the point it generated enough income for her to quit her other job — and she did it all without dipping into her family's capital.

THINGS ARE NEVER AS GOOD AS THEY SEEM -- OR AS BAD AS THEY SEEM

THINGS ARE NEVER AS GOOD AS THEY SEEM -- OR AS BAD AS THEY SEEM

This doesn't need much elaboration. It's just that you should always remember that your mind can easily play tricks on you.

When everything seems rosy, enjoy your success — but don't rest on your laurels! Be assured there are always new challenges just around the corner. You never know what troubles are brewing even when all seems perfect. You may not see your troubles — or won't allow yourself to. So, don't slack up when things are going well. This is the perfect time to keep building on what you have to protect and strengthen it. Never take your good fortune for granted!

Conversely, when the outlook is black, there are innumerable lines of defense you can retreat to, but which your mind won't even let you think about until you are faced with the necessity to do so.

When you are faced with a set of extremely bad problems, there is no need to panic. Sit down, think the unthinkable, come up with a viable disaster control plan, implement it, and move ahead from there!

Bryant's lawn care business was booming — his crews were working a lot of overtime to keep up with all the contracts, and Bryant was thinking about cutting back on marketing efforts. But his partner Ben insisted on continuing to develop new business, even though it meant a lot of evening and afternoon work for both of them. Then their largest commercial client unexpectedly terminated their services due to an internal change of management. Fortunately, Ben already had the marketing momentum going, so he simply built upon that to bring in new business. Within 2 months, the company had replaced all the lost revenue, without having to lay off a single employee.

Never Solve A Non-Problem

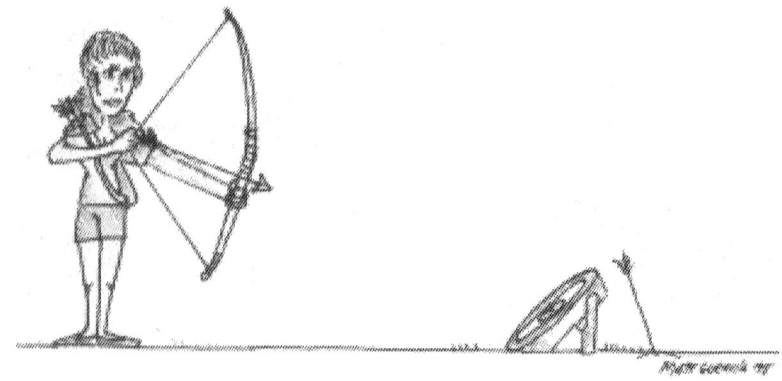

IF YOU AIM LOW YOU WILL HIT LOW

IF YOU AIM LOW YOU WILL HIT LOW

As you set goals for yourself and your company, consider the risk of setting your goals too low. It may be human nature to be cautious in order to not expose yourself to failure. If you set your goals low enough, then you will most certainly succeed — in short changing yourself and your company. On the other end of the spectrum is the enthusiastic manager who is always challenging himself and his people to do better. He sets goals high and works hard to achieve them. This second kind of manager may often miss is goals — so, to one way of thought, he might appear to be less successful than a manager who sets and meets more cautious goals. But you can be assured that the second manager will consistently achieve higher goals and results than the first one.

You and every manager in your company must aim high. Be realistic, but aim high. The manager who plans to simply survive will stand still ... and eventually not survive. Ultimate failure is assured.

Carl and Jacob were asked to set sales goals for the coming year for their respective groups. Carl set a target of increasing revenues by 15%, while Jacob challenged his group with a goal at three times that amount — an ambitious 45% increase. By the end of the year, Carl's group had increased sales by 20%, beating their projections. Jacob's group increased sales by 40% — and missed their goal. When it came time to hand out bonuses, guess which group came out ahead? The one who met its goals? Or the group whose sales increase was double that of the other's?

COMPROMISE IS BAD

COMPROMISE IS BAD

As a manager, you will be confronted from time to time with internal conflicts. Rule number one to remember is never compromise — or you'll have two unhappy people.

When two groups or two individuals are in conflict with each other, make those involved aware that you will make a decision for them if they cannot sort it out among themselves. This might be all that is needed to convince them to find a resolution.

If this doesn't work, and the conflict is brought to you for a decision, listen carefully to both sides — and then make a decision for one side or the other.

Follow-up will be key. Have individual discussions with those involved about the benefits of being a graceful loser and a graceful winner. Don't allow the loser to chip away at your position to the detriment of the organization. And don't allow the winner to gloat over his or her perceived coup. Attempt to get them both on track and back on the same side.

John and Peter both wanted the newly vacant position of head of the art department. Their boss, not wanting to disappoint either, proposed they become co-heads of the department. It only took a few months for her to regret her decision. The other members of the department began complaining to her because of conflicting priorities. John would give an art director a project, only to have Peter pull the art director off it to work on another assignment. Then when John's job was late, there was hell to pay all around. The boss asked Peter and John to find a solution — fast. John agreed to relinquish the job to Peter. Peter, in exchange, agreed to let John have creative control over his own projects.

KEEP YOUR PROMISES

KEEP YOUR PROMISES

It is natural, especially when building a business, to want to promise your customers the stars and the moon. Don't do it. Only promise what you know for sure you can do.

It is better to disappoint a customer by saying no than to say yes and then not be able to come through for them. When asked about a deadline, ask for time to think. Always build in a buffer zone, and then, if you can, deliver ahead of schedule.

Always put yourself in a position to deliver more than promised, never less.

When a regular customer called in a last-minute holiday order for 100 poinsettias to Genna's flower shop, she was tempted to take the order. But Genna knew it would probably not be possible to locate that many poinsettias in the time allotted. With her apologies, she had to decline the order, even though she knew the customer would be a little annoyed. He was, and went to her competitor to place his order. The competitor, who had the same doubts as Jenna, nonetheless guaranteed she could fill his request. However, the owner of the second flower shop had to call the customer on the day the flowers were due to deliver the bad news: she couldn't fill the order. The customer was then truly annoyed because he had been misled by the second owner. He became one of Genna's long-term customers, because he knew her word was always good.

ONLY ORGANIZE ESSENTIAL MEETINGS

ONLY ORGANIZE ESSENTIAL MEETINGS

It's a real talent to hold a good meeting. Many of them are colossal time-wasters. Usually, the fewer the meetings and the smaller the attendance, the better.

Don't have a meeting unless you have a specific task to accomplish.

Only invite those people who are vital to accomplishing that task.

Limit the time — have a definite start and finish time. Then, start as scheduled, and when the allotted time is up, adjourn the meeting.

If a summary of the meeting is to be written and distributed, it should be done by the senior person at the meeting — they'll carry much more weight that way.

The new president of XYZ Corporation instituted a weekly staff meeting to keep all division and department heads informed. Every Tuesday at 9 am on the dot, the meeting started, no matter who was or was not there. In fact, attendance was optional. The format was simple, but direct: starting at one end of the table, each individual made a brief report on problems and developments. Issues requiring more attention were dealt with by assigning the right people to get together to discuss later. Those without significant news simply passed when their turn came. The meeting always ended by 9:45 — sometimes sooner. By 5pm that day, the president had dictated and distributed a one-page synopsis of the meeting. Everyone agreed it was the most productive time of the entire work week.

THE BEST MANAGERS ARE
THE BEST COACHES

THE BEST MANAGERS ARE THE BEST COACHES

If you're going to be a great manager, you've got to be willing to do whatever it takes to help your players advance toward the goal. You'll act as blocking back when needed, run interference between them and any unreasonable demands of the owners, identify objectives and give every member of the team the right training and tools to meet those objectives. No task is too menial if it means helping the team move forward — you'll type a new draft, you'll stay late to help assemble a presentation, you'll get the powers-that-be to approve a project.

The best managers see themselves as playing coaches — the first on the field and the last to leave. The best managers are always available — to give the go-ahead, to suggest an alternative course of action, to circumvent a major mistake, to supply information. If he or she isn't there, the rest of the team can easily get frustrated, lose momentum or even give up.

When Elaine was promoted to manager, she decided she had finally earned the right to ease up on her workload. She was great at setting goals and assigning tasks, but she was often unavailable to answer questions or oversee the execution of the tasks. Late one evening, her staff was putting together an important proposal for Elaine to deliver the next morning when they discovered several key pieces of information were missing. Elaine did not answer her phone at home, and no one on the staff had her mobile number. Tired and aggravated, they finally had to abandon the proposal half-finished. When Elaine arrived the next morning just in time to pick up the document and dash out the door to her meeting, the staff grimly informed her the proposal was not ready. Elaine had to reschedule her appointment. Meanwhile, a competitor's proposal for the same piece of business was accepted.

**KEEP ALL CONFLICT
EYEBALL TO EYEBALL**

KEEP ALL CONFLICT
EYEBALL TO EYEBALL

Honest disagreement is healthy. If conflict is constantly suppressed, you'll frustrate those who may actually have some great ideas for change. You have to give your people a forum for speaking their mind, venting their frustrations, and fighting for their beliefs.

In a healthy organization, employees should feel comfortable openly disagreeing with each other — and with the boss. Your job as a manager is to make sure conflict is productive. Don't let it get to the point where it's consuming the energies of your people. Instead, encourage open, honest discussion and resolution of differences. Make sure everyone keeps in mind the purpose: not to tear each other down, but to build a stronger organization.

Kevin was a young man full of ideas, many of them good. He saw a lot of things in his organization that he thought could be improved. But rather than approach his coworkers or his supervisor, he took his ideas to his supervisor's supervisor — sending emails or requesting meetings sometimes several times each week to complain about various problems. Instead of the welcome response he expected, Kevin was perceived as a troublemaker by the supervisor. When his coworkers got wind of his actions, they became rather chilly toward him for not first confronting them with his complaints. Kevin soon left the organization, having learned a lesson the hard way. In his second job, he was still full of ideas — but found he had much more success discussing them openly with his coworkers.

MANAGE BY WANDERING AROUND

MANAGE BY WANDERING AROUND

The best managers are seldom found in their offices. Instead, you'll find them out and about — talking to people, checking the progress of a project asking questions, listening to ideas, complaints, suggestions.

Make yourself accessible to your people. Get out and see what's happening. Cover all your territory. Make sure your people know you are there to see and to listen. And use the opportunity to keep them informed, too. Let people know what's going on in other parts of the company, especially concerning things which are important to them.

Don't be a recluse in an ivory tower. Get out among your people on a regular, informal and spontaneous basis.

Whenever David Ogilvy wanted to talk with one of the associates in his large advertising agency, he did not summon them to his office. Rather, he went to speak to them in their office. This kept him visible to his many associates, and also helped to keep him in touch with the day-to-day workings of his business.

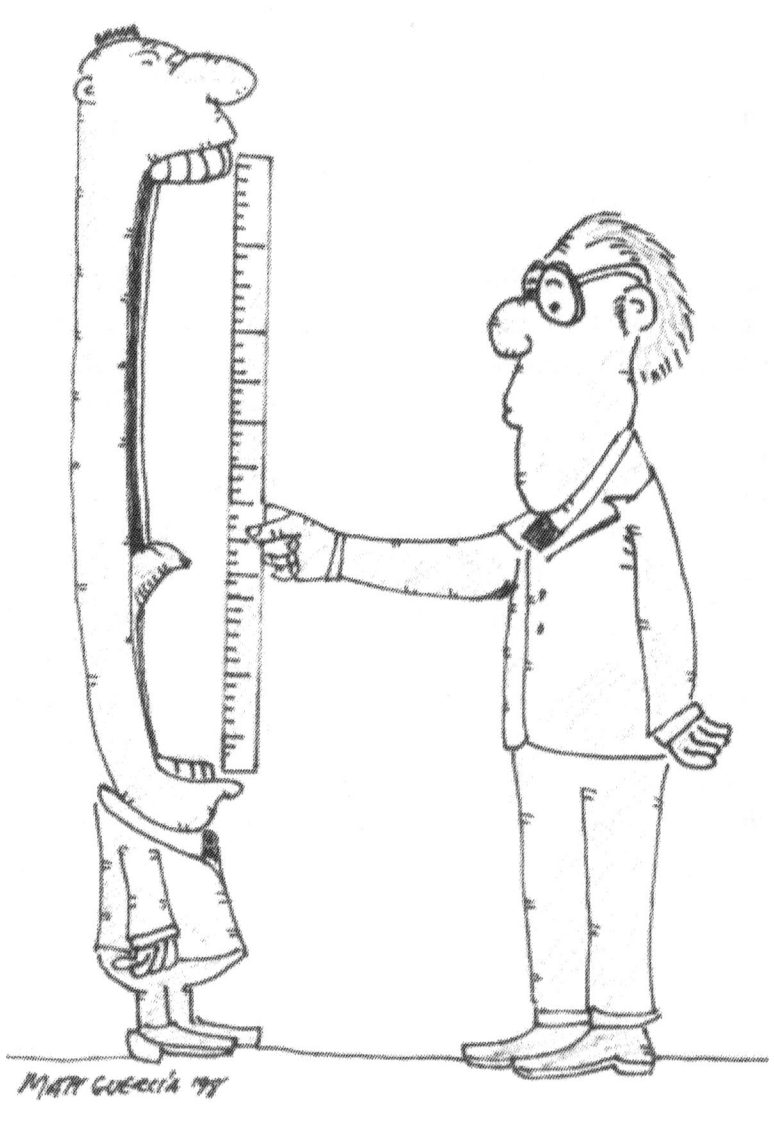

DON'T BITE OFF
MORE THAN YOU CAN CHEW

DON'T BITE OFF MORE THAN YOU CAN CHEW

Lucky is the person who is being used to the best and highest use and profitable is the company who has those people. One of the biggest wastes in business is not under-utilizing staff. Rather, it is giving people assignments far beyond their abilities. In the first case, the work will at least get done. In the second, nothing gets accomplished.

Encourage your people to work up to their potential, but don't guarantee failure by promoting them above their heads, or assigning them tasks that are too difficult. Challenging people to do their best is good. Expecting them to do the impossible is disheartening for them and wasteful for the company.

In a large, bureaucratic organization, raises and promotions happened like clockwork. You could expect to steadily advance if you stayed with the company. As years went by, however, the system of automatic advances actually proved to weaken the company. A large number of employees had advanced to positions that were actually far beyond their capabilities. The company was top-heavy with people with years of seniority but lacked the leadership and skills in many key positions.

MAKE EVERY DECISION AS IF YOU OWNED THE COMPANY

MAKE EVERY DECISION AS IF YOU OWNED THE COMPANY

Imagine if every individual in a company made every decision as if he or she owned the company.

How might a receptionist respond differently to a difficult client if she were considering the impact on sales? Would expense reports look different if the individuals making them acted as though the costs were coming out of their own pocket? How would "owning" the merchandise affect the way stock clerks handled it? How much more mentoring might occur if senior employees saw the bigger picture from an owner's perspective?

There are tremendous advantages gained when one takes "ownership" in his or her job. You can go to work for just yourself, or you can go to work for the company. If you're at the right company, the latter will allow you to grow and share in the success of the firm. Indeed, working like you own the company is one way to insure that one day you just might.

George's business was in an industry where competition was fierce and margins were slim. He knew the key to success was to somehow inspire employees to work as hard as he did. When a new employee joined the firm, he or she received a personal orientation from George; where he shared his vision of the company and its future with the new employee, offered unlimited access to training and mentoring, and guaranteed that those who worked to build the business would reap the benefits. Putting his money where his mouth was, George also offered employees a way to earn stock in the company. Because he was able to inspire employees to take responsibility for the company as owners, he gained a loyal staff of people who treated the company like it belonged to them – and all did well because of it.

SHARE REWARDS AMONG EVERYONE IN THE COMPANY

SHARE REWARDS AMONG EVERYONE IN THE COMPANY

Owning stock has traditionally been one of the perks of the executive elite. Historically, stock options have been reserved for on the top 1/10 of one percent — in other words, only one of a thousand workers.

This is backwards thinking. Why deny one of the most powerful incentives for performance from the vast majority of your employees? Make more of your people owners!

You'll probably encounter some resistance from the purse string holders in your company when you broach the subject. But the deeper into your organization you can spread ownership, the bigger your returns.

Spreading the wealth is great for young, growing businesses. And the benefits of employee ownership never end. Many big, mature and successful companies became fat and lethargic at some point, but employee ownership is one way to circumvent this. One of the reasons Sears is doing so well today is because almost 60 percent of their people own shares in the company through Sears' Employees' Profit Sharing Fund. This holding, worth more than $2 billion, averages out to more than $10,000 per participant. That's a lot of motivation!

For years, the stock in a large accounting firm had been held by a handful of senior-level executives. When the company was having trouble retaining talented people, the board tried a new tactic: every single employee was eligible to earn shares of the company stock through service and performance. Attrition practically disappeared, and company profits grew as every member of the firm truly had a stake in its success.

REMEMBER THE 90/10 RULE

REMEMBER THE 90/10 RULE

In most human activity, 10% of the effort produces 90% of the results. Also, 10% of the activities produce 90% of the costs. In other words, the activities that produce most of the results are generally not the same as the activities that produce most of the costs. Sometimes the percentages are 80/20, or similar, but the principle still holds.

Control your business. Cutting accounts receivable and unbilled revenue in half could have a greater and more immediate impact on profit than bringing in new business.

The notion that if you watch the pennies the dollars will take care themselves is nonsense! Instead, you can reap enormous payoffs by controlling the few items that are gobbling up most of your money and time, and by paying close attention to the few things that are producing most of your profit.

Robert was a freelance editor always overwhelmed with projects. He typically had dozens of smaller, low-paying assignments for every large and lucrative one. His standard approach was to work through the small assignments to "clear off his desk" so he could devote his undivided attention to big projects. But invariably, small assignments just kept coming in, so that Robert never got to the large jobs. So Robert tried a new approach: each week, he tackled the biggest assignment first, then worked his way through any smaller ones he had time for. His income increased dramatically when he began focusing his attention on the projects that would bring him the highest return.

CONTINUALLY LOOK FOR DETERIORA-
TION AND THEN CORRECT IT

CONTINUALLY LOOK FOR DETERIORATION AND THEN CORRECT IT

Building a business is like building a sandcastle. It is falling apart even while you are building it. You must constantly both repair *and* build.

In business, deterioration is a continuous process, and is very difficult to perceive when you are in daily contact with it. The world is changing rapidly. The services and products that made the company might not be the ones that will take you into the future.

It seems to be a law of nature that human enterprises, so bustling when new, drift toward stagnation, with talent and labor increasingly devoted to activities of little opportunity.

It is the entrepreneur's job to reverse the normal drift. Continually look for deterioration and then correct it! Focus the business on opportunity and away from problems. Regularly reevaluate. Look at your business with new eyes every day. Apply constant effort to correct and adapt effectively to an ever-changing present.

The Swanson family had owned a small urban grocery store for more than 40 years. The first generation had made a fine living by catering to the large, traditional families who lived within walking distance. They were known for fair prices and a good selection of basic items used in cooking family meals. But through the years, the neighborhood changed dramatically. Families moved out to the suburbs, and young professional couples began to move in. The second generation of Swanson grocers realized these new shoppers — upwardly mobile professionals — were more interested in convenience foods, in variety and in gourmet and ethnic fare. The grocers continuously adapted their product offering to cater to the new customer base, and thrived while other small grocery stores went under.

HOMILIES ON PEOPLE

SUCCESSFUL PEOPLE SUCCEED DES-
PITE HOW EVERYONE ELSE SCREWS UP

SUCCESSFUL PEOPLE SUCCEED DESPITE HOW EVERYONE ELSE SCREWS UP

Have you ever noticed that with most unsuccessful people, it is never their fault? Someone else always does something wrong, which causes them to fail in what they are doing.

On the other hand, people who are successful succeed in spite of how everyone else screws up!

If you blame your failures on someone else, then what you're admitting is your success is dependent on someone else.

But you can spot the winners in any endeavor. They admit their own mistakes and learn from them. They place the responsibility for their success exactly where it belongs – on their own shoulders. In their own hands.

Nothing – and no one – is going to stand in the way of their success.

Jack and Will each had a major presentation to a prospect, and depended upon the marketing department to provide key materials for their meetings. Unfortunately, the presentation materials were sorely lacking, and neither Jack nor Will won an order. Jack complained back at the office that he lost the order because the marketing department made such a lousy job of the presentation. But Will explained to his boss that he lost the order because he didn't concentrate enough on what the marketing department was preparing. Which one do you think has a better chance of winning an order next time?

NEVER, EVER BE AFRAID TO HIRE SOMEONE AS GOOD OR BETTER THAN YOU ARE

NEVER, EVER BE AFRAID TO HIRE SOMEONE AS GOOD OR BETTER THAN YOU ARE

This is the most serious mistake an entrepreneur can ever make.

If you are afraid of high-powered people, don't even try to be an entrepreneur. You started the company, you have equity, and of course you are going to share rewards among your people and partners. So what is there to be afraid of? *Mediocrity* is the thing to be afraid of.

Once you hire the best people, pay them as much as you can – even if it's more than you're making at the moment. *So what?* Great people produce great results – watch them help your net worth increase.

David Olgilvy, founder of one of the world's largest advertising agencies, firmly believed having subordinates is a great mistake. To illustrate this point, he once gave his partners a set of Russian dolls, the kind where several successively smaller dolls fit into each other. In the smallest doll he enclosed a message warning against hiring subordinates. The message was clear: Hire "down" and that's the direction your business will go. Hire "up" and watch it grow!

John was at a crossroads. He knew in order for his small architectural firm to compete for a higher level of work, he would have to bring on board an architect with much more experience than himself – and pay this person considerably more than himself. John bit the bullet and hired one of the best architects in the city. The gamble paid off: thanks to the dynamic presentation prepared by the new architect, John's firm landed its biggest project ever.

IT'S BETTER TO BET ON PEOPLE THAN IDEAS

IT'S BETTER TO BET ON PEOPLE THAN IDEAS

Great ideas in the hands of ineffective people always amount to nothing. It is a mistake to invest in a company or a technology where the people aren't strong enough to make it effective. On the other hand, there have been numerous successes where the idea wasn't earth shattering or the technology wasn't rocket science, but where the people were absolutely brilliant.

Of course, the best of all possible worlds is that powerful idea in the hands of incredible people with the ability to implement and sell, and the dedication and determination to pull it off. Every venture capital firm in the world is in search of this wonderful combination.

Bottom line: people drive success, not ideas. If you love the idea, but have any doubts whatsoever about the people – don't get involved.

Tom, a venture capitalist, had met with the two principals of a start-up company, and was impressed. They knew their stuff, had produced a good plan, and Tom was seriously considering investing in their company. To learn more, Tom took the team, eight people in all, out for a social drink. Within an hour, he had changed his mind about the company. The two principals were not leaders – they were martinets, telling the team what to do, what to say, keeping two of them from even speaking at all. The company exists today, funded by another investor ... and struggles with an annual staff turnover rate in excess of 50 percent.

IF YOU'RE NOT HAVING FUN, YOU SHOULD PROBABLY BE LOOKING FOR A DIFFERENT JOB

IF YOU'RE NOT HAVING FUN, YOU SHOULD PROBABLY BE LOOKING FOR A DIFFERENT JOB

Should work be fun? Absolutely! Life is simply too short to be squandered on activities you don't enjoy. Also, you cannot consistently do a good job if you don't really like what you're doing. That's not fair to you, and it's not fair to the people who work with you.

Of course, any job has aspects that may not be especially enjoyable. And, everyone goes through periods when problems stack up and even a great job is, at the moment, anything but fun. Get through your difficulties and get back to having fun.

On the other hand, if over the long run you generally are not enjoying your work, you have little chance of being consistently successful. In that case, sticking to a job you don't like is a disservice to everyone — especially to yourself. Your lackluster performance can cause extra work for others. Your dissatisfaction can infect others and create even more discontent and unhappiness.

Look around you. The most successful people are the ones most likely to inspire confidence and happiness in others. They're the ones having fun.

Pressured by her parents, Reagan pursued her law degree and practiced law for the first ten years of her career. Her real passion, photography, was relegated to her spare time. At age 35, Reagan realized her legal career had stalled, despite the fact she was quite competent. After much soul-searching, Reagan resigned to take an apprenticeship position with a local photographer. By age 40, she owned her own studio, and had achieved both artistic and monetary success in the endeavor she loved.

POOR PERFORMERS CAN AND MUST BE FIRED

POOR PERFORMERS CAN AND MUST BE FIRED

Occasionally, a poor performer can be turned around. But if an employee does not quickly work to overcome his or her deficiencies, let them go.

Your good performers could probably work around poor performers. But it comes at the expense of extra energy on their part — and often, extra aggravation. Why penalize your good people?

Poor performers are a drag on morale as well as profits. Be gracious, be fair — but weed out poor performers on a regular basis if you want your other people, and your business, to thrive.

In his small insurance agency, Jon was known for his soft heart. So he found it difficult to let the receptionist go, even though his agents complained she often misdirected mail and forgot to pass on important messages. Jon kept giving her "one more" chance. After several months, two of his best agents grew frustrated and left. Belatedly, Jon realized he had sacrificed his better people — and untold business opportunities — for a poor performer.

NEVER BE AFRAID TO PAY SOMEONE
MORE THAN YOURSELF

NEVER BE AFRAID TO PAY SOMEONE MORE THAN YOURSELF

Hire the best people you can, pay them what they're worth, and your business (and your income) will grow.

If your best salesperson goes great guns and earns commissions far in excess of what you're paying yourself — terrific! That's what you want!

Paying good people good salaries is one of the best investments you can make. The best incentive compensation scale slides up, not down.

On their best months, at least 2 or 3 of Lee's top salespeople earn commissions in excess of his own salary as owner of an art gallery. Far from being distressed, he is delighted at the situation. For now, he continues to reinvest the income they generate for the gallery back into the business. Lee knows that in the long run he'll profit handsomely from having — and paying for — the top salespeople in town.

YOU CAN NEVER TRAIN SOMEONE TO BE WHAT THEY ARE NOT

YOU CAN NEVER TRAIN SOMEONE TO BE WHAT THEY ARE NOT

A shy person can memorize lines, but that won't make her an actor. Any one can learn the tactics of football, but only a few will ever play in the NFL.

Training is valuable, but it cannot overcome basic personality characteristics, ingrained attitudes, or make up for the lack of natural abilities. Training can't convince an overly cautious person to become a risk taker, nor can it turn a born pessimist into an optimist. It won't turn a musician into a manager, and vice versa.

What training *can* do is provide knowledge to an individual who is open to receive it, and has the attitude and aptitude to use it. Hands-on training is the best of all, because it provides the opportunity to practice and develop the skills needed to put the new knowledge into use.

Heather's design business was barely breaking even, despite the fact she had lots of business, and worked long hours. She wasted valuable hours every day dealing with an unorganized office and a nonexistent filing system. She even suspected she was losing money due to her lax billing system. In desperation, Heather hired a business consultant to train her to organize and run her business better. While the consultant imparted valuable knowledge to Heather, nothing changed. Heather understood the problems, she simply had neither the inclination nor the natural aptitude to solve them. Then the consultant suggested another tactic: hire a part-time employee to do all the non-design work — the scheduling, organizing, billing and so forth. Heather retained the consultant to hire and train the new employee. Within six months, Heather's company began to turn a profit.

HOMILIES ON MAKING SALES

THINK IN TERMS OF CUSTOMER SATISFACTION...

NOT IN TERMS OF SERIVCES OR PRODUCTS

THINK IN TERMS OF CUSTOMER SATISFACTION NOT IN TERMS OF SERVICES OR PRODUCTS

It's not so important what your selling ... what's important is what your customer is buying. Indeed, customers rarely buy what we think we are selling to them. We may think we're selling a product or a service – but what they are buying are the satisfactions they'll derive from their purchase.

Are you selling wool socks? Or the promise of warm feet? If you're selling cellular phone service, you may be selling flexibility to a businesswoman, but peace of mind to a mother. Carpenters want quarter-inch holes, not quarter-inch drill bits.

And no one buys a Rolex just to tell the time.

Make the effort to find out your prospects' needs and expectations. Uncover and understand their satisfactions, or "hot buttons." (You might be surprised what you learn!)

When you can identify the need – and then *satisfy* it – your product or service will sell.

Feeling on top of the world after passing the bar, and with his dream job offered to him, Steven decided to reward himself with a new car befitting his new status as an associate with the most prestigious law firm in town. He had narrowed his choice of cars down to two, and paid a visit to each dealer. The first dealer dutifully informed Steven of all the fine features of the automobile, from anti-lock breaks to extended warranty. The second dealer, after getting to know Steven, focused his sales pitch on the stylish image of the car, on the luxury of its appointments, and congratulated him on arriving at a time in his life when he deserved such a fine automobile. Guess which car Steven purchased?

GO FISHING FIRST ON YOUR OWN TRAPLINE

GO FISHING FIRST ON YOUR OWN TRAPLINE

A trapline person is any person in a potential customer organization who is in a position to either place an order with you, or introduce you to someone in the same organization who can. The first orders in most successful start-ups are trapline orders. It is amazing how many companies have gotten off the ground not so much from an original idea, but because the people starting them realized their contacts in business were extensive enough to obtain the initial orders to get things rolling.

For long-term objectives, it is often necessary to talk of market size and market share, but in the short term, it is essential to talk of orders, and the best way to secure orders is to think in terms of people who can place these orders – and quickly. Make a list of your contacts and follow up on it – you'll find having your phone call taken by someone you know sure beats making the dreaded cold call!

People buy from people. As your company grows, ask your customers to refer you to others. The trapline process is a continuous process which demands discipline; use it no matter how large you grow.

As part of the business plan for a new venture, the partners made a list of every individual they knew personally who could either contract work to them, or refer them to someone who could. Then the partners made personal phone calls to their contacts, seeking sales or sales leads. As new people came into the firm, the trapline process was expanded through them and their contacts. The company secured several early sales through those initial personal contacts, and continued to grow the business by utilizing the trapline process.

OLD CUSTOMERS NEED LOVE TOO

OLD CUSTOMERS NEED LOVE TOO

While it is essential to seek and continuously acquire new customers, it is just as important to pay attention to your current and past clients. One of the greatest mistakes we can make in marketing and selling is in the sin of neglect.

Taking your bread-and-butter clients for granted is a sin which is hard to forgive in business. The customer may well have been buying from you for a long time, pays his bills on time and seldom complains, so why not leave him alone? After all, getting new business is exciting and extremely challenging, so this activity receives all our attention.

However, long-standing customers are the easiest to upset by neglect exactly because of the length of association. Newer ones don't get so upset. And don't forget – while you are neglecting any customer, your competitors are trying to impress and win business from them. Make it hard for anyone in your business to even get to see your customers! Do this by creating a marketing plan for your existing customers – visit them, call them constantly update and contact them. In the service industry this constant contact equals increased business – business which is the easiest to get because you and your customer know and trust each other.

All customers need love, but your old and current customers need the most. After all, they are the source of your current revenue. Love will ensure they are continuing contributor to your company's success – shower them with it!

When his company was young, Bill obtained the first customers. As the company grew, Bill turned much of the day-to-day contact with those customers over to other people. However, he made it a point to have face-to-face contact with each and every customer on a regular basis – checking to make sure they were happy, prospecting for new business. His original customers are still the backbone of his business, because Bill never forgot they were the most important ones of all – and he never missed an opportunity to make them feel that way.

NEVER PROMOTE YOUR
TOP SALESPERSON

NEVER PROMOTE YOUR TOP SALESPERSON

Your top salesperson has exceeded her quota by a factor of two for three years running. Is it time to make her a manager?

The offer of promotion may be flattering, may appeal to his or her ego, but for the truly great salesperson, it is not what he or she needs. Nor is it a good idea for your business.

If you truly want to reward a great sales person, do one or all of three things.

First, provide a budget to expand his empire. Ten to one he won't recruit other good salespeople – his ego won't stand it. But, he will hire support people to do the work he hates and allow him to concentrate on selling.

Second, increase incentives. Give more commissions, money and shares.

And thirdly, promote her to the board if possible. It's great for others in the company to know they can reach the top not just by having the largest head count in people, but by having the largest head count in customers.

John loved the freedom of being a new business sales man. Granted, he was always late with his reports, and missed his share of internal meetings, but he always produced double quota figures. Ignoring his strengths and trying to correct his weaknesses, his boss promoted John to sales manager. The result? Sales lagged. What the boss should have done was give John an assistant to do the paperwork, organize meetings around him as much as possible and provide John with rewards, instead of headaches, for doing a great job at sales.

LISTEN

LISTEN

It can be difficult when you are all action and enthusiasm, talking and leading, to actually sit down and listen. Even more difficult is to listen properly.

Listen and *hear* what your customers want. Tune in closely to understand what motivates your customer and what benefits he or she wants to buy.

Listen to your people, their ideas, their grievances, and their hopes and aspirations. On these you can act.

To hone your skills, do a post-mortem on a meeting. Tape it, play it back and time how much time you spent talking vs. listening. Or during a conversation, try the old tactic of restating what you've just heard, asking the other person to confirm that you understood them properly.

Jerry was developing a direct mail campaign to help increase a client's business. But after an internal presentation of the campaign, a few of the salespeople told Jerry the problem was not so much a lack of leads, which the campaign was designed to generate, but a lack of sales materials to convert leads to sales. When Jerry truly listened, he realized that without solid sales materials to back up the sales team, his direct mail campaign would fail. He redirected his efforts to provide the client what they truly needed. With the new sales materials Jerry created, the client increased business by developing current contacts. The satisfied client was then happy to invest more with jerry's company to develop a direct mail campaign to increase business even further.

HIGH VALUES = HIGH PRICES

HIGH VALUES = HIGH PRICES

John Ruskin supposedly said, "There is hardly anything in the world that some man cannot make a little worse and sell a little cheaper, and the people who consider price only are this man's lawful prey."

You have to have confidence that your product or service is of value, and that the right customer will realize it — and be prepared to pay for it.

You will always encounter customers who tell you your price is too high. They probably would not buy anything from you at any price. They only tell you this because it is easier or less embarrassing than to tell you the real reason they won't or can't buy. Don't fall for it.

Any entrepreneur who undertakes to reduce price by reducing either quality or profit seriously undermines the entire company.

The business strategy of performing shoddy work for a cheap price is a strategy for disaster for obvious reasons. The strategy of taking a reduction in profit is also unacceptable. For one thing, if you gave away all your profit, you wouldn't reduce your price by a very large percentage. More importantly, without a profit a company is meaningless to shareholders. Without a profit, a company will die.

Never accept a job that can't produce excellent results for the price obtained and still yield a good health profit.

A backpack designer decided to increase his profits by using a lower grade fabric. However, the stores experienced a high rate of return because the backpacks' fabric ripped easily. The designer not only lost all his profit on return debits to his account, but also lost the respect of the store buyers, adversely impacting future business.

ALWAYS CONCENTRATE ENOUGH
RESOURCES ON NARROW ENOUGH
TARGETS

ALWAYS CONCENTRATE ENOUGH RESOURCES ON NARROW ENOUGH TARGETS

Ahh, the power of concentration. It's an absolutely essential power to master if you want to be successful.

A showshoe is designed to spread the weight of a person over such a large area that it has virtually no impact on snow. In the same way, there are people who splinter their time into so many different activities they don't really succeed at any of them.

Yet something as seemingly soft as water has the power to cut through stone — when all of the energy of a falling stream is focused continuously on one area.

Concentrating on what you are really best at can dramatically increase your effectiveness. Don't squander your resources by spreading them too thinly. Instead, select the best opportunities so that you are sure to punch through. Limit their number, narrow their scope, and concentrate all your resources on them. You'll increase the probability of success and maximize your profit.

Giovanni had developed a loyal clientele at his restaurant, Bella Cafe. His guests loved the personal touch he gave to the place — Giovanni was in the kitchen every night, either cooking or overseeing every item that was served. He spent time talking to his guests, and often prepared custom meals for regular patrons. A local investor, seeing the restaurant's success, came to Giovanni to propose franchising Bella Cafe. Giovanni wisely declined. He knew that in the competitive Italian restaurant market, what made Bella Cafe stand out was the emphasis he put on building relationships with customers, and his willingness to cater to individual tastes. It wasn't something he felt he could replicate over a chain of cafes. Instead, he focused his attention on his one restaurant — and kept it steadily growing and profitable.

WHEN YOU HIT ON SOMETHING THAT WORKS, WORK THE HELL OUT OF IT

WHEN YOU HIT ON SOMETHING THAT WORKS, WORK THE HELL OUT OF IT

This marketing principle is extremely important — and easy to overlook. After all, many successful people are also creative, and it's natural to always be going on to something new. However, success – and profit — comes not from just developing a winning service or product, but from selling it again and again and again.

Look around. Is there something you should be systematically exploiting? If repetition bores you to death, find someone who enjoys routine to help you out. There are some very capable people who enjoy doing the same thing over and over again.

A related concept is the notion of developing a product or service that will keep making money for you even when you're not working at it. Think of it as developing one or more "oil wells" that will keep pumping for you, when you're asleep, when you're on vacation, even after you retire. Invest the time to develop product or service loyalty; seek out those kinds of products that can bring monthly fees or other revenue pouring in for a long time.

A large computer company had a policy that when they came across a "vein of ore" they didn't pass it by to keep looking for the best vein in the whole mountain. Rather, they continued their exploration, but also stopped and mined the vein at hand for all it was worth. Some of their products weren't the greatest in the market, but they sold thousands and thousands of them, year after year. The company? IBM.

KNOW YOUR COMPETITION

KNOW YOUR COMPETITION

Not knowing what your competition is up to has blindsided many a corporation.

Make it your business to know what they're doing. Only then can you plan against, market against, advertise against your competition. Only then can you beat them to the punch with a new idea or a new product.

When Shannon opened her housecleaning business, she brought a major asset with her: three years working as a housecleaner for a competitor. She knew intimately the services offered (and not offered) by her competition, and she also had firsthand knowledge of customers' chief likes and dislikes. So she designed her business to fill in some of the gaps in service offered by her competitor, and was able to build a solid business.

NEVER ACT LIKE A LEADER

NEVER ACT LIKE A LEADER

That is to say, don't act like a lot of the so-called "leaders" who are at the helm of many organizations today — the ones who are simply following the rules and getting the masses to follow them also.

A real leader knows how to get his or her people to consistently turn in superior performances. They've learned an important secret: true leadership must benefit the followers, not merely enrich the leaders. True leaders allow others to shine. They're behind their people, not in front of them.

True leaders take care of their people first. In combat, officers eat last.

True leaders share their vision. They "infect" others with enthusiasm. They inspire and uplift.

True leaders empower their people. The philosopher Lao-tsu expresses it this way: "When the best leader's work is done the people say, 'We did it ourselves!'"

One sales group in a large division consistently outperformed all the others. The division manager was interested to learn why. From his perspective, the leader of the group appeared to be just an average manager — not the hot shot you might expect. The division manager got a big clue when he went to visit the offices and saw that the staff's computers and phones were much more sophisticated than the standard company-issue equipment. It seems the group leader had been plowing back all his discretionary funds into upgrading his staff's equipment — rather than outfitting a fancy manager's office or leasing a new car every six months. This was one leader who knew the value of "feeding" his troops first.

MARKETING IS WAR

MARKETING IS WAR

We've all been taught that marketing means satisfying the needs of our customers. But what if your competitors are already doing that?

Marketing is war, and the competition is the enemy. You must out-strategize, outmaneuver, outwit and overpower your competition if you are to win the battle — and the customer.

Having a better product puts the odds on your side, but it won't win the war for you. You have to outflank your competition to win the minds, the hearts, the loyalty and the business of your customers.

You've got to get there first, with the most firepower.

Keep in mind that you're not just marketing a product — you are continually marketing against something — against the competition, against perception, against lack of awareness of your product. Keep your defense and your offense up at all times — attack the competition and protect your own position.

There is a national pizza chain who has at its helm the former CEO of another, more established pizza chain. In their advertisements, the CEO claims he joined the new company because he "found a better pizza." He's not just selling the benefits of his new pizza— he's waging a full-out war on the competition in the mind of the customer. It's a gutsy — and highly persuasive — message.

ATTACK YOUR COMPETITION WHERE HE'S STRONG

ATTACK YOUR COMPETITION WHERE HE'S STRONG

Don't just look for weak points. They very likely aren't important to begin with. Instead, examine your competition's strong suit, and find a small spot where you can drive in a wedge.

Example: When Hertz was beating the pants off Avis, the folks at Avis came up with a brilliant advertising campaign which encouraged customers to "Rent from Avis. The line at our counter is shorter."

Avis had attacked a weakness inherent in Hertz's position as the leader.

Likewise, look for areas where your competition is strong — that's something that obviously has merit to it. Then find a way to turn their advantage to your own advantage.

As tourism began to grow in a picturesque village in the Blue Ridge foothills, several new hotels were constructed to take advantage of the burgeoning business. They stressed their modern facilities and brand new rooms. A traditional country inn that had been in business for two generations came up with just the right strategy to compete against the new hotels. They kept guests coming to the inn in droves with a refreshingly candid and incontestable marketing pitch: The Chestnut Inn. Older Than The Hills.

BEWARE
THE MARKETING DEPARTMENT

BEWARE
THE MARKETING DEPARTMENT

Beware the attitude that allows marketing to become departmentalized and thus compartmentalized into some mysterious machination occurring down at the end of the hall.

Marketing has to be mainstreamed into everyday operations. It should be a primary force in your company, and it should be handled by the front line.

On regular occasions throughout the year, the boss and a group of key people, along with a few folks from your ad agency and your controller's office, should retreat for some serious reflection and discussion. Review and scrutinize the basic elements of your marketing: Who are we selling to? What are we selling? And so forth.

Bring back your best ideas and solutions and put them into play. The work you do at these meetings and every day of the year will prove to be more fruitful than the decisions that come down from an isolated marketing department.

At a company-sponsored retreat of a computer service firm, the question was asked: "What are we selling?" When the response given was "keeping clients up and running," the head of scheduling had an issue with that promise. He reported that on several occasions customers who called in Friday afternoon with a problem were aggravated even if a technician could be out at 7 am the following Monday, most particularly those companies where employees often or always worked through weekends. The boss made an immediate decision to allocate the resources to have repair technicians on call every weekend, and directed the advertising agency to begin work on an ad campaign touting the new 7-day-a-week availability.

FIND A SEGMENT OF THE MARKET SMALL ENOUGH TO DEFEND

FIND A SEGMENT OF THE MARKET SMALL ENOUGH TO DEFEND

In other words, become a big fish in a small pond.

Try to pick a segment small enough you can dominate it. You will never be bigger than Pizza Hut. But if you concentrate on tailoring your pizza restaurants to local tastes, you could be bigger than Pizza Hut — in your market.

Find a segment — be it geographic, volume, a niche product or market — that a larger company will find difficult to attack. That's where you can concentrate your energies and become big.

Resist the natural temptation to try to grab it all — instead, study your competition, analyze the market, and pick a segment small enough that you can dominate it.

A large music chain dominated the city's market for CD sales. It was nearly impossible for an independent to compete against their prices or wide selection. Instead, a local music store leased a space just off campus of the city university and concentrated on classical music and other selections that catered to the needs of music majors. The store had a tiny share of the overall music sales in the city, but garnered the lion's share of the college market, which was ample to make it very profitable.

THE MOST IMPORTANT CORPORATE IMAGE IS A HAPPY CUSTOMER

THE MOST IMPORTANT CORPORATE IMAGE IS A HAPPY CUSTOMER

Fortunes have been spent by corporations in the pursuit of creating a corporate "image."

Teams of "experts" busy themselves creating campaigns, speeches, reports designed to project this image onto the customer's mind.

What you should really concerned about is what the customer thinks about your company, not about your company's advertising. You should care what he thinks about your product, not your logo. Rather than being so concerned about the image portrayed in your annual report, you should focus on the numbers contained therein.

Make your customers happy with a great product and great service. Make your employees happy by sharing the profits. Your image will take care of itself.

Evolution was a hip cafe with retro decor, in-your-face ads and all the other elements that defined a "cool" image. Employees dressed in the latest fashions, and the food was trendy. In its early weeks of business, the town was abuzz about the place. However, for all the effort that went into designing the perfect look, very little attention was paid to quality control in the kitchen or adequate training of the wait staff. While the exciting advertising generated new customers, there was virtually no return business, and word-of-mouth business was nil. Within 6 months, the cafe was out of business.

DIRECT MOST OF YOUR ATTENTION
OUTWARD RATHER THAN INWARD

DIRECT MOST OF YOUR ATTENTION OUTWARD RATHER THAN INWARD

In a sales organization, the best managers are rarely in their offices. When they are, they are usually on the phone. The reason is simple: no one inside the company is buying!

So reason number one to focus your attention outside the organization is because that's where the customers are.

Reason number two is to seek out new employees. You don't want to build your staff by pirating good people from other departments, and you certainly don't want their deadwood.

A third reason to focus your attention outside is that in a good business, you cannot get ahead by beating an associate out of his job. If that's how it's done where you work, you should consider changing jobs. And don't let that be the m.o. in any company you manage.

Attend to your internal duties, but always keep your focus outside, where the big opportunities lie. And as for any "bloodthirsty" instincts — focus them at your competitors, not your coworkers.

Charles spent the majority of his time at his new sales position ingratiating himself to his supervisors. He lunched with them, prepared special reports for them, was always at his desk before they arrived. Spencer, on the other hand, concentrated his time on customers. He spent the minimum time required to complete necessary paperwork. He spent time in his customers' offices, instead of his own. When a merger necessitated the downsizing of the sales force, personnel decisions were made purely on sales performance. Spencer, not surprisingly, kept his position, while Charles was given notice.

NEVER TRY TO SELL THE CUSTOMER YOUR PET PROJECT. SELL HIM WHAT HE THINKS HE NEEDS

NEVER TRY TO SELL THE CUSTOMER YOUR PET PROJECT. SELL HIM WHAT HE THINKS HE NEEDS

It's natural – in fact, necessary — to get excited about your latest and greatest product or service. But it's a mistake to try to sell it to the customer just because you're in love with it.

You can use your pet project, and other successful projects as a way to open the door or establish credibility. But if your customer isn't jumping right on the bandwagon, pause. Ask questions. Find out about his needs and problems. Listen and be sensitive.

After you have been filled in by the customer, ask him what kind of help he thinks would be useful to him. If he doesn't reply with anything specific, you should at least now know enough to think creatively — from the customer's point of view — of ways you could help him. When the customer does have something specific in mind, you are in luck because he's already convinced he needs it.

When you try to sell the customer what he tells you he needs, you'll find your success rate will be high, indeed.

Heather was all set to sell the local university on her company's new accounting software. But after a probing interview with the buyer, she realized that the accounting department was actually functioning fine —it was the admissions department that was horribly antiquated. She gathered enough information to go back to her software designers, who proposed a package that would automate much of the admission's staff workload. She was able to secure a major design fee for her company and a nice retainer to help convert the admissions department to the new system.

HOMILIES ON FIGURES

PLAN TO MAKE A PROFIT
RELENTLESSLY AND IN DETAIL

PLAN TO MAKE A PROFIT RELENTLESSLY AND IN DETAIL

In business, you make a profit for the year by making a profit for the quarter; to make a profit for the quarter, you make a profit for the month; to make a profit for the month, you make a profit for the week. And so forth.

Every day that you do not put forth effort is a day gone for good. You'll have to work twice as hard the following day to make up for it. Trying to play catch-up is not an enviable position to be in.

If you can focus on the details, you can affect the larger outcome. Every action you take either adds to, or takes away from, the bottom line.

Make today count, and tomorrow, and tomorrow. Make each week count, and each month, and each quarter. Do this relentlessly, and you'll be pleased with your results and year-end.

When a mail-order company installed a new computer system, major complications ensued, and the company's ordering system was out of commission for more than a week. Although the employees put in an incredible effort once the system was back up and operating, it was more than 2 months before the company's orders were back to normal. The lost revenue, of course, could never be recaptured.

NEVER PAY THE WINDOW STICKER PRICE

NEVER PAY THE WINDOW STICKER PRICE

When someone asks you to pay a price for their product or services, this is the maximum they expect you to pay. Negotiate!

The easiest way to give your profit away is to pay the asking price. Ask for a discount. Ask for "commercial" rates. Shop around! Your customers probably do it to you. And have you noticed that the larger the company is, the harder they often negotiate? So think like a big company – and you could become one, too. Every dollar you save goes into your cash flow and profit. Every dollar you spend goes straight into someone else's. Don't be afraid to ask for a discount, and don't be soft-hearted.

Of course, you should expect to pay a fair rate for products and services. Just be smart about it. Consider possible incentives you could offer to encourage a lower fee, like a guaranteed volume of orders, for example. Make the relationship win-win, beginning with asking for the right price.

Jenny, the CEO of a small software company, needed a job done by an independent contractor. She selected one contractor she knew could do the job. He was the best, but he was asking $120 an hour, which she could not afford. Jenny offered $80 an hour – plus a percentage of the revenue from the resultant product for a period of three months. Her offer was accepted. She not only saved her company a considerable sum on the development costs, but probably accelerated that development with a brilliant job being done because the contractor had the incentive Jenny was smart enough to offer.

LIMIT YOUR TARGETS TO
HIGH-VALUE ITEMS

LIMIT YOUR TARGETS TO HIGH-VALUE ITEMS

Every company and every individual has limits on resources. There are only so many hours in a day, only so many dollars to be invested. Complicating matters are the eternal distractions, the never-ending stream of unimportant tasks that can divert you away from the ones that matter.

The choice is yours. To be successful, you will have to learn to ignore the distractions, and concentrate on the tasks and opportunities that have the highest potential for return.

Every week, rank order your priorities and rank order them in order of immediate high value to your company. Remember the 90/10 rule. Remember you cannot do most things. Any manager that sets most important things to do this month and in turn list these in order of importance to the company stands a far better chance of succeeding than a manager who list all the thing that need to be done in a random order and systematically works through that list, in the order that they are written.

Mary religiously sat down every Sunday evening and went through her sales prospects. Every week she ranked divided them in order of closing dates. Every week she closed an order. Every Sunday Gargao sat down and religiously made a list of everything he had to do that week. He finished and won an order a month.

BUSINESS IS NOT A HUNDRED YARDS DASH, IT'S A MARATHON THAT NEVER ENDS

BUSINESS IS NOT A HUNDRED YARDS DASH, IT'S A MARATHON THAT NEVER ENDS

Some people are great at the 100-yard dash, but fail at long-distance. And business is more like a never-ending long-distance run. You can never quit.

Landing a new contract — or any other kind of success — is like winning the 100-yard dash. You feel exhilarated and proud. But if you don't get up the next morning and start running again, you're going to fall behind. Success must be pursued constantly.

Endurance is key. You need as much zeal at the completion of a task as at the beginning — because the task of succeeding never ends. Learn to get up every day and do it again. And again. And again. Dogged determination will take you much further than sprinting all out and then taking it easy.

Don't assume you have it made after a few initial successes. You make your success day after day after day.

Cindy's catering business, which had garnered a small but loyal following for imaginative food and presentation, got its big break when the firm was asked to cater the mayor's inaugural ball. Business poured in after that great success, attracted by the fresh ideas Cindy had brought to the affair. Cindy and her staff could hardly keep up with the workload; in fact, they were so busy catering events they had no time to experiment in the kitchen to create the novel items that were responsible for their success. Over time, Cindy's business began to wane as her fare became less and less original. When the catering for the mayor's ball was awarded to her competitor four years later, Cindy realized she had actually fallen behind by standing still.

THAT'S IT ...
GO MAKE SOME MONEY

EDITOR

Nora Minor graduated with honors form Kent State University with a degree in English and a concentration in American literature and history. She has earned her living as a writer for more than 20 years. She lives with her husband and young daughter in Ormond Beach, Florida.

CARTOONIST

Matt Guercia is a cartoonist and artist living in Seminole, Florida. He specializes in line drawing both in black and white and color. His work has appeared in Family Forum and Cinemagic magazines. Matt is also a talented clay animator who has spent a great deal of time teaching kids the art of animation form clay to computerized. He graduated from the Art Institute of Ft. Lauderdale in Florida.

AUTHOR

Tony Carter is best described as an "Entrepreneurial nanny," someone who likes to take a newborn company, teach it to walk and talk and then go back and do another one. He started his first software company in 1969, sold it and started the European arm of CACI in 1975. In 1981 he was the founder of James Martin Associates, a company he grew to $60M in eight years. Between 1989 and 1995 he undertook various venture capital and start-up related assignments before starting the International Business Group, Virginia's first for profit Internet incubator. The name of the company is now Edge which is involved in I.T., M&A, ventures and incubation.

www.ingramcontent.com/pod-product-compliance
Lightning Source LLC
Chambersburg PA
CBHW020437220526
45464CB00002B/742